To Life from the Shadows

Lamine Pearlheart

OTHER BOOKS BY THE SAME
AUTHOR

The Sunrise Scrolls

***

*The Mayan Twins - At the Edge of
Xibalba's Well*

PREFACE

Through the years I kept note of every personal thought I deemed worth inscribing and they accumulated to form a diverse and rich personal set of sayings and awkward poems.

I tried at first to incorporate them into a fictional book I was working on, but then I thought, "Why would you make the reader go through a lengthy novel if he or she is only interested in some valuable thoughts?"

Selflessly agreeing with myself, I decided to publish them in this form.

I also believe that a short disclaimer is in order, and therefore in this collection you will find that,

No wisdom shall be imparted,
No experience brought about other than that which you have known,
No relief provided other than that, which you are ready to hand over,
No eternal promises of life beyond your current formless, ethereal conception

However, you may seek and find,

Some poorly written poems,
Some attempts at observation,
Incoherent thoughts,
A troubled mind quoting itself and trying to find the light by illuminating others

I hope you find solace in this book and most importantly some light.

CONTENTS

ACKNOWLEDGEMENTS

To all those that made my life beyond poverty and wealth richer,

To all those that made my days brighter,

To all those that helped my continuing to be,

Thank you :)

On Human Limitation

She looked at the row of newly constructed architectural marvels, their architect confident and satisfied, unbeknownst to her, happened to be the man standing next to her, she said to him, "Marvelous indeed; it has no pillars to hold it and changes colors every time I look at it."

She pointed, to the dismay of her interlocutor, to the heavens.

On Hope

No sunset winks, but surely be followed by the sunrise! – Try to remember this in your moments of despair

The Importance of Silence

"Not all that is deep, hidden, needs to be shown; apparent in gravity

Not all that flies needs to come down; true of the stars

Not all that which screams needs to be heard; see the hound dog

Not all that is great is doomed to be subtle; manifest in the tectonic plates frictions." Said the rose.

"Do you believe in God?" Asked the priest.

"No," responded the rose, "My faith, like all that is divine, is on the heavens suspended."

On Agelessness of Being

There comes a time when one is asked, "Is there a time and place you wish to have lived in?"

The fool always pauses, thinks and points to a time and a place.

The wise says "I have!"

On Nationalism

"Where are you from? What is your country?" are some of the most favorite questions of the slaves.

On the Usefulness of Humiliation

Humiliation is not a business I would gladly trade in; I leave it to weaker minds.

A Useful Prayer

"Let me be light where darkness reigns

Let me be a soothing memory there where grief is supreme

Let me be warmth so that the darkened heavens are but passing

Let me see through the veil of distress to view the end and the lifted weight of failure

Let me see my end not as expected but as hoped for"

These are the prayers heard in the wells of souls.

On Temptation and Thrift

"Temptation is a big number." Said a miser.

The Condition

If life were a survey, none would live due to the overbearing assessment

If the world were predictable all would die of anticipation

If the weather were constant all would seek unpredictable elements

If disappointments were the measure of our successes then our failures would find worthier recipients

If heartbreaks were non-existent then humanity would surely die of anguish

If the heavens were always clear and blue then the universe would find no space to fill with its deep creation

If wisdom was imparted to everyone then foolishness would be the sensible currency of the day

If violence were the answer to all of our needs, and not but a cowardly escape, then the reason for viciousness would be a question answered

If time was not a fleeting glimpse, then eternity would seem such a long shot

If you and I were eternal then a question must be answered for each and all; what is from us that merits being timeless?

If fires were set by firemen then of all things water should not be the nemesis

If we are but to survive then living has long sailed away

If material wealth is everything, and not a means to ease some material discomfort, then none is poorer than a rich man

If fluency of tongue were the measure of intelligence then parrots would be the most eloquent creatures and redundancy a sought-after ability

If eloquence of mind were not permitted then authority better seek elsewhere for fulfilment

If hatred is the breeding ground for reason then motivation should not beg for questions

And finally, if I were as bright as these words pretend to make me be then my darkness is but a passing gloom and I an exceptional sunny occurrence

On Isolation

Isolation gives time but not immunity.

Our Age

We live in an age of tailoring and where tailors are almost extinct.

On Greed and Knowledge

It is not good to hoard money and it is equally unsanitary to hoard knowledge; the more you hoard the less you think and the lesser you know.

A Gloomy Perspective

Behind the veil lies a stern island

Behind the stains are metallic tears

Behind the rivers are the unforgiving seas

Across the hillside creeps the night

And between the ruins are you and I

Home of the raven and territory of the sharks

Authority vs. Justice

"You are out of order!" Says authority
"I might be, but you are disorder incarnate!"
Responds justice

On Being Nice and Weakness

Some people think that being nice is a weakness and not a good quality to have; they don't seem to see the sun shining on them every day.

The State of the World

Some nations are but the reflection of an intimate state of being of criminals with their victims.

Your First Months at Work

During your first months at work nothing happens by coincidence; all is planned for you are being weighed and measured.

The Distraction Game

Ah, the distraction game! It is played by everyone: by the child when he changes the subject because daddy would be upset if he knew who broke the windows.

By the artful magician who dazzles us through his fast hands.

Ah! By the scoundrel pack of hyenas avoiding scandals through the unwrapping of a newly found national pride and blaming other realms.

It is meant for us to see the defects of others and distracts us from knowing the real threat; ourselves.

On Evolution

I always find it fascinating that people who believe in the physical evolution of human beings, from apes to humans, find it hard to understand or accept that a person can indeed change from an evil state of mind to one of benevolence.

Armed with their incredulity, they take umbrage and make it a point to go and insult the hopeful religious minds.

On the Need of Inspiration

When I feel down and see things around me that are reprehensible, I raise my head and look up, and I see impeccable conduct and exemplary leaps; that is when I see leadership.

On the State of the Citizenry

There's only one State and that is the state of mind, and one empire; yours over it. Never let anyone take it over.

On Democracy

Democracy is like money; it is fake and unreal, the more people believe in it, the more tangible it becomes until it is the main currency of the kingdom; a fake benevolent form of trade is what it is.

On Leadership

Primary Rule of Leadership:

Leadership knows; it does not believe.

On Everlasting Life

"What if you knew that you will live forever, would you tell anyone?"
"No, I will take it with me to the grave!"
"Aha, but you will not die!"

"Yes, but an everlasting life in prison can be a drag; the envy of the powerful and the destitute can be equally damaging"

Why the Chickens Never Believe in Propaganda

"We are fighting wars for democracy!" Said the radio.

"Democracy? Amongst the wolves, hyenas, and the humans! Yeah right." Thought a chicken once.

The Good Guy vs. the Right Guy

"There's the good guy and the right guy"
"What is the difference?"
"The good guy could be your friendly neighbor, the right guy, well, that's a doctor when you are sick."

On Human Uniqueness

I don't know if there are people like me, I know that there are people better than I, but of me there is and will be only one and for that I am grateful.

On Pretentiousness

You my friend, if you need anything to make you change your mind it is pretentiousness for that is the way of the abyss.

On Being Useful

Sometimes I feel like a robot or better a slot machine, being paid, punching in and out of work.

The only time the cycle breaks is when I learn something new or go out of my way and help someone else and he or she is appreciative, then I feel human again and I am myself.

Politics and Truth

It is very difficult to find the truth in politics and business when the public is considered enemy number one and is the target of all conspiracies.

My Legacy

When everything is gone; of me, I am betting, there will be left a light

There will be rivers of sunrise

Energy I will become

There, parts of my thoughts would stream into the sunlight

On Children

"Children are as close as one can get to the angels." Said an old man.

"Obviously you don't have children." Said a mother.

"They do loose some of their feathers when they reach earth." He responded.

On Elections

"In a dictatorship, every election is faked and everybody seems to know it except for the dictator." Observed a psychologist.

"Thank God we have a democracy." Said the chronicle.

"Yes indeed, for in a democracy it is the politicians that are rigged." Said a homeless person.

The History of Propaganda

In the beginning, there was human, surrounded by fear and presumption, then came propaganda the infant of deceit and reward.

Centuries ago came decorum and the earth is ever since unrecognizable

On the Nature of Death

Does it hurt to be a rock?

I will be buried and that is of me to become; a beacon of things to come.

Does is hurt being air?

This is exactly what I breathe every day giving me life.

Is it scary being a shadow?

Does it not help me see part of myself?

Does it pain being dust? Does it not sparkle golden?

Could it be vain being a spark?

Isn't all we are?

Graduation Day

On his graduation day, he was so happy for he thought to himself that going forward he needed not to think for he had a piece of paper now that said he was smart; years spent studying, his personality reformed, he was finally above the ignorant world far below.

He darted forward, his foot hit the wet puddle as he exited the ceremonial hall, his weight sank while he tried hard, summoning all his powers to calibrate his posture, but it was too late for he hit the pavement of the real-world face on and was unrecognizable even to himself.

The Like

Like shadows we moved

Like rivers we sought shores

Like stars we sank and like beautiful horses aimlessly yet gracefully roamed

Like suns we dived seeking a tomorrow
Like humans we faded

Like lions we were scared of our shadows not recognizing the roar of our limits

Like life we didn't know whence

Like rocks we sank and rose back projected
Like ships we never sailed but floated away

Like poets we did jot rhymes, but loved the feeling of being lost

Like oceans we look up to the seas

Like mountains we cheered up for the tiny mounds

Though the world may bury us and the truth lie to us; safe is our bright past we know unchanged.

Like time we fly with no aid

Like souls we do need no weight

Like diamonds we shine on regardless of the creature that is looking

Like stars we cannot but sparkle

So, listen to the silent voice inside;

Like you are one of a kind

Like urge

Like a surge

There is no key to find

Linked like momentum in time we are

TO LIFE FROM THE SHADOWS

There are no errors in your mind

But your life to unwind

Find the like!

Media

The maniac amazed at his lunacy; that is the status of some of the media today.

Thinking Outside One's Realm

To think about oneself from outside, other than from within, is not a common tradition or practice among nations and individuals; a shot to the ego is what it is.

On Darkness and Light

"It is simple indeed:
You can defeat the shadows by more darkness or with more light, the first will make you a sombre person and the second a brilliant star; water doesn't just put out the fire it can be the source of floodgates."

On Ego

Sometimes the distinction between the good and the bad is so blurred that you don't need your ego to obscure it further.

The Memory of You

For my last breath on this rock as ugly as it may be
A planet of deceit and thunder

I will certainly miss your wonders

Your genuine smile and your caring embrace

Through my last dance on this crowded desert

I will always look for your generous face

As my soul shatters, as my pompous human glitter falls beneath the weight of truthfulness of time

As I slide into oblivion

I will remember you and your sensible ways

I will hold on to the eternity of our past existence

We saw through the lies and covers

Touched by the warmth of a heart seeking no miserable quarters

As I fade, I wish you a more perfect match

In a little while returning to my eternal perils of a motionless silence

I drink to the futility of kings and already fading industry barons and ah, the wily puppeteers!

Always with sympathy for the hunchback fool for in him no malice

The time an all-cunning and vengeful master

As this rock bounces forever never knowing where it is heading

I waltz to the mortal remains of our favorite hours

Never cared much for potential pots of gold or famous stars stricken marbles

Never saw the need of lavish shelters

Tombs fading under the glory of sunlight and the memory of you

On Nations

"Nations you say? Where does this madness come from?

The sun when it rises knows no borders,

The moon when it sets sail knows no privileged harbor,

Death when it comes sees no skin, colors, creed or just banners!

Whence does the illusion spring from?"

Living on Passions Alone

"It is known that one does not get much nourishment if one lives on his or her passions alone."

"Should a blind person be blamed for his or her restricted sightedness?"

"Yes and no!"

"Why?"

"Well, they should be if they want to play with fire."

Two Lovers

They were no lovers of things which make a sublime creature a pity

No star royal rose from the heavens the day they met

No banners were unfolded to greet them

Flowers and roses, gifts to each other, they carted hidden in time

They were not rich for poverty of spirit is an exorbitant price to pay a measure

Poor, they weren't for in the depth of scarcity they carried the spark of generosity

On each other they set the truest bet the day they met

The candles may flicker

The sun may set

But on the day they met it wasn't just a bet

Of the two mortals, the gods in envy stood

For in all their glory as such they could not let go or would

A prime condition of every loving living thing

Two living things, two living things to the divine unintentionally they glowed

A true measure

A beacon to a shattered vessel

The promise of another sailing ship

All that is, is not what seems

All the living things can be

All living things can cease

As they did fall the heavens wept, somber liquids called rivers and embracing expanses hereafter known as seas, mourning their parting afar

Ways of the World

Humankind sometimes behaves in a very lop-sided way; an honest person, with impeccable behavior throughout a lifetime, makes unintentionally an honest mistake and the world rises in uproar and points the finger to the daring criminal.

A known criminal makes a dishonest mistake of being honest and the world applauds, shows its gratitude and enthusiasm obliterating the honest person behind the crowning cheers and applauses bestowed upon the scoundrel.

On Relatives and Tenderness

It is known that a tree gets more sympathy from a bird than from its sturdy brethren

It is known that a rose sees more compassion from a bee than from its colorful sisters

It is a fact that the earth is healed more by the warmth of the sun rather than the attention of its infant the moon

It is observed that the sun is the loneliest amongst billions of related stars

It has been noted that humankind is the antithesis of humanity and that humankind is never just passing by

It is customary for nations to seek havoc and fortune, but not always in the same order

It is the rule that no disorders spring from chaos and that peace is a state of mind

What You Need to See?

Of death: the remaining everlasting bright memories of a precious loved one passing on

Of the sunset: its crumbling beautiful warm light comforting the body and illuminating the soul

Of grief: the lightness of hope and warmth of remembrance piercing the heart with soothing embraces

Of despair: the glow of certainty of the past; its abundance of confident hopeful memories

Life Measured

Once upon the time a man walked miles and miles, and wanted to measure the distance he travelled, but could not, then he started counting the days and realized somehow that he travelled three hundred and sixty-five days; a year in our imperfect measurement.

He then made a resolution that what matters is not the distance travelled but the time and effort one puts into the journey.

Forty years later, just before he passed away, he looked back on his life and was faced with the same dilemma; he could not measure the distances he travelled all his life and he concluded that there was no way he could. He determined that life is not the sum of distances travelled, nor the years lived, but a once in a lifetime an adventure unfathomed.

On his deathbed, his smiled as he saw through the eyes of eternity a silhouette of a child walking and stumbling but always continuing on one direction, and as the child reached his destination, he rested and he, the dying man, could see the face of the infant and realized that it was his life he was looking at.

Humankind

It was said, "You may trust a human, but never humankind." The kind is a rule.

Looking Inside

Did you hear the screaming horizon?

Did you touch the sunset?

Have you perceived the twilight right after the sunrise?

Have you looked at your soul and found it to be cautious?

Have you shivered at its methodical disorder?

Have you made judgement on others and found it well deserving and logical?

Have you weighed your life; measured the essence of your footprints?

Do you always remember how weighted is your discourse of yourself?

Do you see the treachery deep inside your dilemma?

Have you sought vengeance on yourself and did you see it through?

Did you seek equal retribution as you did for others?

On History

World History should not be looked at as a book of accusation or truth; it is neither and will never be as its truths are incriminating subjects to those that hold its weight.

It is a book of warning, and, foremost, that of propositions and complex situations where the student of history is forced to think, question, and possibly provide solutions to theoretical riddles.

History thus viewed would lose its propaganda edge and vanquish the realms of anger and subjectivity to become a laboratory for the students of the subject matter.

Students of history are not participants in its past events, they share not the burden of past generations and should never allow themselves to be hinged by the guilt and culpabilities of its past or presently living actors.

At all cost, they should avoid historical fanaticism for they also are the victims of past botched attempts and half backed solutions; they are never part of the past for the moment they reached legal maturity their present world history starts.

World history is not you, they, them, and is not even I; it is "it" a subject matter and anyone prompting otherwise is under the influence and propagating pure propaganda.

On Change

For centuries grownups went the beach to swim, always swimming the same way, until one day a young girl grabbed a flat piece of wood, she found laying on the beach, and slid it over the waves.

Everyone laughed at her as she fell off her board.

"She made an utter joke of herself!" A person said and many of the experienced swimmers concurred.

Well she, she just smiled.

She tried again, but this time she laid flat on the board, moved up through the waves, stood up facing the sunset in front of her, her hands extended like the wings of a phoenix, she rose through, what looked like a liquid fire, and tamed the ocean.

She darted up and surfed.

The people of earth never viewed the beach the same way again.

The moral of the tale: because something has been done the same way all the time does not necessarily mean that there is no room for improvement or change.

That Which is Left

Of me an idea to survive the wreckages of time

To fly above the downtrodden horizon and come back in endless rays; warmth to the rescue of the frozen veins

To revive and console

To heal and find new ways of growth; soothing voices to the echoes of silence and purging rain

Of me a memory of all that is dear; precious like a sunrise and endless as a sunset mourning the passing of the day

I am energy when expiring coming back in charging waves

Sweeping across the world clearly refined

Of my passing through time, a dying galaxy lighting the lost travelers unseen

The lightness of wisdom, of goodness invisible

A humble earth reflection of the wondrous lights above and about; a womb teeming with life lost in the desert space

Like angels after an eternity returning home tired yet willing to do more

The Weight of Imagination

When logic is not enough, one must use imagination.

Our Time

When the truth comes through mouths of the sharks

When the void is the only spark

What if the rogues are the ones leading us so far?

When disaster calls your name, and if it all were the same!

When planes crash in mid-air

When the horizon is your own demise

When soft words are split in half to be shared like precious bread crumbs in a century of starvation

When everything moves up, but there is no elevation

When saints hide afraid of salvation

When monsters cry tears of negation

These are the times we live in

On Capitalism

Capitalism, the only economic system that ever was, has created sophisticated societies and individuals who know how to appear to do and say the right things, within set frames, without any belief in the intrinsic values of goodness.

Capitalism has produced sophisticated individuals with no regards to civilization for a capitalist person is sophisticated and not civilized.

This product is a vessel with no soul; a perfect mirror of nowhere and nothingness.

This system killed Sapiens and replaced him with an authoritative ape; this ape by design hates and lacks humanity; it worships Moloch, the owner of things, and lives to senselessly consume. - *A warning to societies with agrarian values: stay away from fascism and communism!*

On Trusting

"Don't trust anyone." Say people who must know themselves to be untrustworthy.

The Riddle

I sell that which I don't buy

I harness the horses that I couldn't ride

I live by the flow of the sea that I don't understand

I summon the names of the people that long ago, I've known to be true

I climb the seas the way I descend the disguising mountains in the sky

I rule not by virtue but by the virtue

I hide not due to fear but to find surprising adventures

I wash my sins in the helplessness of humankind

I muck about for the sake of not stumbling upon

I woo the Universe to find my own place in the maze

I hold the sails tight not to go far

I measure the skill of my survival by the artfulness of my denials

I see far, but all the time hold my head down, for the fools to think consternated I am shutting down

I walk and walk, but I don't seem to reach places for the purpose of my walk is to meditate not to lose grounds

I never praise but shed light on that which illuminates

Who am I?

On the Inherent Nature of Goodness

One does not impose nobility of spirit.

The Contrast

To find without to look

To hear without to listen

To hide without to fear

To hail without to kneel

To catch and still be able to throw

To feel without to amputate

To crawl, yet still to walk

To chant and yet still know how to sing

And that is the river that is the flow

There is the light there is the dark

On the Absurd

The intelligent are usually silenced by the absurd not by the stupid as many think

A Backgrounder

Within the rose in the tomb, there rests my unbalance,

The answer to my scattered offences

Homoconsomus

Modern humans have killed the ancient myth of the gods and replaced it with that of limitless unquestionable consumption.

On Tyranny's Outrage

It sends its sons to the scaffold, and when they come back bloodied, Rome asks why?

On Poverty and Richness

Extreme richness breeds cruelty while extreme poverty breeds arrogance.

On Puppets and Puppeteers

But we all know that the goats have no religion, that the wolves live in packs, and that the hyenas are the true owners!

On Love

Love doesn't need a container; love doesn't need a whiner

Love stands by itself

Love doesn't need a protocol, doesn't need coal, it burns with gravity and it is alight by mystery

Ablaze not by fire, but by hearts that do expire

Love doesn't need a warehouse; love is not given but found

Love is not the limit

Love is not a town, not sarcasm, nor a clown

Love is suicide, suicide of your soul, of your brain of your chances to run

And all I care about is suicide

Love is madness a train full of rails spread with each step

A further heartbeat of your sadness

Love is a barbed wire, a cemetery and fire

And all I care about is to be ablaze and part of the quagmire

Love is highway, the crossroad of your desires

Love is attire and I do want to be dressed

Love is an exception; a heavenly touch and I need the miracle

Love is an impact, a preview of death

All I wish for is a heart attack

Love is a mad house and am the homeless of your touch

Love is your fantasies and I need you

Love is a kiss and embrace, love is with or without a trace

Love is I holding your face

An endless dance and I am willing to build the fence

Love is a helpless bliss, and I am praying for your kiss

Love is a sense and I jumped

Love!

On Wisdom

To be wise is to look without to feel, and then when they feel, then they look and see what you've felt and then, only then you are wise to be, even though you are no more!

Across

Across the world and over the horizon, under the table and over the deal

Inside the timber and beyond the flames, a part of the world and amid the palms

Deep down my heart and inside my brain lives the acrobat who is I

Just near the wind and close to the door, flying over the world and crushing unto space, hides the truth in its face

Near the abyss and against the world, ahead of tragedy and forward

On the Benevolence of Our Leaders

"It is not that I am a genius, it is that you are idiots." – *This is what I always hear whenever I listen to politicians speak.*

He Who Looks

He doesn't look forward; he doesn't look back, left nor right

How does he look like?

He looks beyond.

On Seeing Beyond

To see beyond one's humanity is what is beyond most people and their pretensions; this is the time difference of the wise to the rest of the population, it is his objectivity, his arrow, his raison d'être.

Without this he is but an imbecile searching for his crown.

Beyond the masses and all that makes noise, one produces a symphony beyond even those who claim to be of it; it reveals itself in the darkness and obscurity not only to the blind, but to those who see.

On Knowledge and Thought

Specialized discipline of knowledge versus a systematic thought approach to knowledge; both never lead to wisdom.

First Lessons of Love

Love dies if it has no more ground to conquer and suffocates if it has too many spaces.

On Life and Death

Hanging between heaven and earth and wondering what to do?

Enjoy the view!

Spaces

Spaces on earth, spaces in space

Spaces without meaning, space with reasons, spaces lost

Spaces recovered, spaces made spaces to cover

Spaces to trade, spaces to remember and some to dismember

Memory to surrender, questions of destiny to wonder

Spaces with age, answers offended, spaces falling without measures

Spaces endeared, spaces like treasures

Spaces on earth, spaces in space

Spaces crawling, spaces just space

Spaces sad, spaces don't show their space

Spaces die spaces; spaces become faces

Spaces to kiss spaces, to embrace

The Generosity of Oneself

Some questions that I ask myself or pretend to ask myself while avoiding them:

"Why is it that my linen is always cleaner than that of the rest? Why am I perfect or rather less perfect, but more so than the others?"

On Being Prepared

To know in order not to be disoriented,
To be able to seize the sense of the event,
To avoid a mental anarchy, and to act effectively

Little Things

If the kiss was a friend

If the time as an enemy

Of me in between

If the kiss was a destiny

If the humans were free and the souls in chains

Off the dust, off the cost of history

Of our names as an anonymity

To Those Expecting Things Not to Change

A tree that is never shaking by the wind is a dead tree!

A Vision

Sunset by the river

River by the ocean

Time by the wind

Echoes by the sound

Whispers in the voice

Touch of your face

A spirit uncovered by a veil

On Humanity's Self-Centeredness

You are like that thunder, which thinks it is the center of the universe and goes on roaring.

On Time to Yourself

Aimlessly walking the world, he was approached by a pretty maid, "You are crazy!" She said.

"So are the birds." Said he.

On Brilliant Minds

They are like the sun doomed in the dark.

On Freedom

Your freedom ends where any other human being's freedom ends; at yourself.

On Honesty

He who says the truth is not necessarily truthful

The World of Man

"The grave, I am afraid, would be tender for my life was a living hell!" Said honesty after taking a look at the world of humankind.

On the Multitude

I have observed that the dogs even when in packs are no wolves, they are alone even if they are many, and that the rivers cannot make a sea even if they are old.

On Giving and Taking

The poor should know how to give; the rich should learn how to take with grace.

On War

I rose and fell, saw the race

Enraged beings idling in a maze

All sides point to an endless craze

Creatures seeking refuge slaughtering the weak underneath a haze

Pompous scruples shed as fast as a torch ablaze

Here and there tatters of a promise soon to be defaced

Recognition of eminence

Humankind shepherded by a psychopathic urge

All points to the gutters' surge

Past and present a wild herd

Sheep and wolves enraged dancing on the fresh carcass of a bird

All hail and follow
All hide and swallow

No hope for a change

On Self-Control

Don't let your chains be your only form of restraint or retention!

Everyone and Everything

Every dog has a name

Every tree carries a stain

Every song its tongue

Every soul has a hole

Like every turn has its curve

Into any age has blown the moon

On Old Age

Old age is meant to slow us down just before the final destination; otherwise reaching the stop would be too abrupt.

On Personal Experience

It is a wisdom that springs from itself like the candles and stars, and it dies by the death of its bearer

No hand can hold it, no words can translate it, and if it did everything would change.

On Delusion

Some people seem to have a vested interest in their delusion.

On Personal Growth

Lady, I help you deliver your thoughts but you always have to raise your own kids.

On Parenting

The role of the parents is not to become the child, but to provide guidance to it, to walk it through the same abyss the parents walked through, but with the help of a light called parental guidance.

Things Left Undefined

The truth - who found it?

Lies - who ever invented them?

Time - who ever superseded it?

Light - who doctored it?

Life - what is the cost?

Souls - what do they know?

Minds - which way please?

Self - talk about luck

Yes - what is it for?

Symptoms they come and go, then they disappear

Wise shouldn't be talked

Temples hide the human inside

Words - what do they say?

Wind - does it really blow?

Sun - what is it?

Help - can we be ready?

Roses - who will buy them?

Sons - who do they cover?

Mothers - who brought them here?

Shades - where do they hide?

Fatigue - how come it is everywhere?

Life - what is the cost?

Memory - will it remember?

Names - who do they call?

A Knight - does he need to ride?

Silence - can you still hear it?

So many - is still a number

Things I Know

I have no future as I never cared for presumption; I smile not to laugh at the world, but to ease its sanity.

The Anatomy of Truth

The truth is sometimes of the one who carries it.

Ways to Find Yourself

Shallow is of the nature of the coral reefs

Echoes are sometimes the measure of the deep

Why Slavery Endures

It is easier for people to accept slavery if they realize that they actually have paid for it.

On Honor

We do not negotiate one's honor, and when we do, it means we have none left and it is better to look for something else.

On Education and Ignorance

Some are wonderfully educated but highly ignorant

On Communication

A picture says more than a thousand words, but a thousand pictures won't say a word

The Origin of Things

Carnivals are made to celebrate

Laughter was invented to hide the buffoon's sadness

History was intended to mark and label people

The States were made because there was nothing to stop them from being

The odds are numbered by the amount of luck and misfortune remembered

The past was introduced to fool the vindictive

The age was a recourse to excuse the fading memory

The temples were built to bury people alive and they still do

The ransom was an amount to be paid not to borrow

Banks have no friends yet are reliable

A bank you don't sit on it; it sits on you

Goodwill is still to be watered

The unknown was a place to forget yet memory is treacherous

Social order is equal plus injustice

Warm wine is a nice drink but too much messes with your neighbor's wife

The Pope came once to my hometown he had to be confessed

Grandmas are as old as they get

The Rain will fall as long as we don't need it

On History Books

History books in the hands of the state are but manuals of hate.

Who Would?

Who would know the river if we are not allowed to speak its name?

Who would know the sunset if the sunset were to hide its colors?

Who would know the tempest and appreciate its force if it were tamed and ordered to stay home?

Who would caress the moon and acknowledge its beauty if he is told to hide underground for the sake of fear?

Who would know the past if its monuments are destroyed, told they have never existed and not to ask how come?

Who would know who he is, if he is constantly told who they are?

Who would want peace if he were eternally kicked in the guts and told he is not worth one?

Who wouldn't fear the wild dogs if they weren't kept on a leash?

On Action

You are asking me how I found my treasures. I never asked I just did; it is wartime and I am Hannibal!

On Hate

Hate, just like love, is a propulsion force; it is also, to the unwise, a defining matter.

Modern Propaganda

Negation by affirmation is one of the vested arts of propaganda.

My Official Position

I am like the sun; I am everywhere and nowhere, I illuminate everyone and none.

On Vagueness

Vagueness, just like the realm of mysterious details, is also the kingdom of the devil.

On Terrorism

Piracy, just like any other form of state terror is always state sponsored, and when it isn't it is tolerated on purpose even though the pirate himself sometimes does not know it.

On Hypocrisy

A group of people with decent non-threatening looks walk on a straight line; one of the members smiling in beatitude, looks like a pious leader, precedes carrying a weighty religious symbol over his shoulder and is steadily moving forward guiding the congregation to what seems to be the commencing of a service.

A kid, catching up to speed, follows behind in a short distance with encouragement from his father who looks back with furtive paternal gazes filled with satisfaction at the continuous short steps of his child.

A disabled elderly woman looks on from a window of a house, overlooking a hill and the scene below, her eyes blinded by the starry reflection of the sun on the expensive chain of the leader, sighs and says, "Nothing like being able to walk heading toward the temple in the

Lord's Day; a just man heading for a just cause."

Truth and Vanity

Between pseudo-truth and vanity; I chose sanity.

On Money

Money is good weapon against the scum and is of no consequence to the noble mind

On Love and Reasoning

Love with no brains is like a bird with no eyes; it can fly, but it can't fly.

On Government Surveillance

Even the most tamed herd can rage in a stampede against the most skilled farmer if left unchecked and is startled; thus, unintentionally destroying all in its path including the farm, which hitherto seemed, to the passive eyes of the lamb, as an unassailable fortress.

The Rebel

I am the Sarasin to the threatening Christian

The Vandal to the belligerent Roman

The Khmer to the Rouge

The Everest and freedom to the newly crowned pompous king

The rain to the unforgiving sun

The olive tree to the cruel soldiers

I'm the ship bringing tidings of truth to the unheeding usurper

The sunset to the eternal presumption of humankind

The humble and simple life to the Bund of superfluous jewelers

I'm the threat of the thinking sparks to the stagnant moisture of the closed mind of authority

I'm the pending truth to every revolution

I'm measure of distress to the impenetrable fortresses

The human frailty, the stubborn consistency of the will of humankind to the egregious time

I'm karma to the resurrection

I'm Saturn to the heights of Jerusalem

A galaxy to the spitefulness of planets

I am just passing by

On Parity

Even amongst our unelected elite one can clearly see that there are some more elected than others.

On Survival

If you want to continue to play, never become a pawn!

On Truth and Timing

In a world starving for validity, the truth, when spoken at the right moment, can be one of the purest and most helpful forms of charity.

On Pomp

A highly secured convoy moved through Main Street carrying what looked like important dignitaries heading to a convention center.

"This must be the leader and his prime minister!" A bystander noted.

"No these are dogs in chains." Countered a wise man who pointed out to the bodyguards and added, "they have to be kept in line!"

An infant holding his parent's hand asked, "What is that in the horizon dad?"

"Man! Kind looks like!" Uttered a broken voice out of nowhere.

On War and Personal Finances

War is the biggest tax hike ever. If this were properly understood, many would stop warring.

On Ambiguity as a Strategy

The power of ambiguity is used as a psychological strategy of inference targeting the opposed in order to render local or foreign subjects' acceptance more likely to come; since they have been informed via rumors, unofficially, they are less surprised and more likely to be amenable after doubt has achieved its gnawing work.

Ambiguity as such can also be a used as a tool of information, once the noise is filtered, on of what is coming down the pipes.

On History and Government

History is not important because it is factual, the truth of the matter is that history would not know the truth even if it hits it in the head as it is all lies anyway, but the importance of history lies in the complex situations it conjures up and asks the terrible question of how would you handle them? It is a fact that all past, present, possibly future as well, governments do lie to their people about the past; heck the past is being written as we speak.

The reason for the continuous lies is that all regimes have stakes in the present and a dimmed population that does not ask questions serves them better than one that stands up and fights back all the way.

This brings us to one of most important question which is, wait for it; is government your best friend? Is any government a friend at all? If you answered yes, then you have not heard a word I said so far, if you answered no then there is hope for you, but you are still wrong, and there is one possible answer which is; it all depends on how amiable it is to you.

On the Pompous Illusions of Nobility

The horse may have the nobility of carrying the king on his back and may look down on other animals, but as far as the crown is concerned he is still part of the livestock.

Rocky Beds, Sandy Beaches

Rocky beds, sandy beaches

Roses on the turf, lingering looks on the surf

Whirring sound from the sea above

Tantalizing shows of seagulls dancing and looking for their abode

Cozy breeze and the smell of the salty load

Mid-day, it is the day the only way

Pretty beach waiting for her princes and lazy prince

Contemplating, it is falling in love with the haze

Pretty beach waiting for the prince to lose his feet and become a leech

Rocky beds and worldwide reaches

The sun is going and all that will be left would be the breach and delusion

Ends all is left and leaves won't cover

Of all built and all seen will be rubble

Rocky beds and sandy sands

On Being in Love

"Love the illicit infant of an imbecile." Said an ascetic person.

"It is the best thing that happened to me!" Says I.

Our Leaders' Constant Message

"Please, let us relive our lies in what we tell you to believe in!" Is what our leaders seem to tell us.

On Being Content

I am not yet told I have a lethal ailment, I am not yet aware of my imminent end; I walk the streets and I see beautiful women and smiling laughing children.

The sun is shining and not a bit overbearing; let me enjoy my blissful ignorance for now as this is all we mortals seem to have.

On Doing Your Part

I do not know what truths you say I speak of; all I know is that I use my torch to see where I am heading, and it is up to you to illuminate yourself.

On the Hidden Government

The corporate farmer and his shepherds do not fight in front of the herd, not that they care what it thinks, but it just so happens that they do not frequent the same establishment as the herd; their disagreements are always in an office, somewhere in the mansion, away from the dull eyes of the sheep.

On History and the People

History is entertainment for the wise and a confirmation for the doomed.

On History's Inherent Details

"You look at the building from the top and you are distracted by the view and you do not feel it leaning. I, on the other hand see it from the bottom up, I am an outsider, and see the weak foundation and I can tell you it is not that sturdy."

On Openness of Mind

"Keep your eyes open and hear everyone; you do not know where the truth is coming from or from whose mouth it will spring up shattering your world."

On Stubbornness

"Listening is one of my best features; I listen to what people say, I do what I want and I then throw it back at them." Said the echo.

On Government

"An elephant constantly in denial."

On Bullshit

Like any other matter of public consumption bullshit is meant primarily to satisfy the hunger of its manufacturer, for you have to believe in your own delusion in order to make people have a share in it.

On War and Longevity

War is a lethal distraction.

On Fear and Hate

Fear and hate: hate is meant to distract from the obvious lack of courage of its proponent; fear, well fear is just a recurring ambivalence.

On the Human Folly

Those who want to sink will surely seek and find an impending shipwreck.

The Delinquencies of Journalism

"Reducing a nation, its women and wonderful children; whole families to a headline. Who dares do that?"

"A journalist"

On Uncomfortable Associations

Never borrow the devil's pitchfork for he will surely use it against you.

On Assisted Societies

There exist societies which are so structured, thus to avoid mediocrity, and which end up not recognizing it even as it becomes an overwhelming trait.

On Domestication

Civil wars, just like the reign of terror, are but the accelerated domestication of a people by the covert powers.

On the Lack of Respect

Insults and the lack of respect are the highest prescribed degrees of the imbecilic and the cowards.

Altruism and Nations

Altruism is a fine ideal that should be encouraged in the individual, yet it is a sign of premature extinction for a nation.

How Democracy Works?

Democracy works for everybody, but it also works for some more than the others.

Things that Religion Never Imparted

Every religion is a blasphemy against the Creator because it pretends to manifest and justify the Divine.

Every religion is a blasphemy against humanity because it pretends not to know it.

On Decency and Friendship

With few decent people who needs friends?

On Looking Back

Denying the past is like spitting on the waves that brought us here.

On Crime and Deterrence

"Does the act of incarceration work as deterrent against crime?"

"No act can be a deterrent as long as the need or desperation to offend is greater."

On Stability

Land to seafarers and those lost at sea is like an answer to a prayer.

For those that never prayed, it is the birth of an enlightening thought after a journey in the ravaged sea of the human mind; a mix of hope and relief, a discovery.

On Staying the Same

He looked to the sky and back to the ground, fixating on the horizon for a while, and then said, "It is like pretending that an honest person swimming amid hungry sharks would get out of the water dry and unscathed."

On Self-Restraint

Doing stupid things, does not make you stupid, but shows how reckless you can be.

By the same token committing a crime does not make you a criminal, but makes you of a higher and expensive liability to mankind.

It shows that you are dangerous with increased antisocial tendencies, and a precarious lack of self-restraint; both equally dangerous to you and the world around you.

On Mother Nature

Kids are a constant well of ingratitude to the eyes of the parents and one has to have the same wisdom of mother earth towards humankind to continue to love and hold them.

On Manhood and Womanhood

Manhood and womanhood are not measured by the number of partners one had, but by the sum of meaningful relationships achieved; just like the quality of a book is not measured by the number of pages it contains, nor is the writer by the amount of books published, but by that ultimate masterpieces created.

On Sacrifice

Soldiers should not be considered martyrs, but brave individuals, when aware of the dangers and still persevere in their march facing a lethal enemy, for no one goes to war thinking he or she is going to die; there is always a faint hope that life will ultimately make it beyond the death fields.

The Dangers of Extreme Poverty and Wealth

The poor proclaim that they do make war because of injustice and misery and therefore for the lack of money, the rich on the other hand to keep what they have or to add to their riches; both are equally desperate and dangerous.

On Revolutions

You say that you have different principles, and yet you still want to live in the same manner. Worst you advocate death and preach the same lair.

On the Last Hour

"What would you have as a last meal if you knew that you would die in the next hours?" Asked a muse.

"Well I will have as ultimate meal a fast." Quickly responded a philosopher.

"What about you?"

"The scent of an old book." Said a poet.

"I almost forgot to ask you!"

"The loving eyes of my beautiful companion." Said the fool looking off to the turquoise sea.

On Choosing Your Words Carefully

The people may not know what you do, but they might know what you say.

What you say is what ruins you the most, not knowing what to say is a lethal disease for a diplomat; a scrupulous step for the arrogant.

On Arrogance

To debase oneself and call one's fellow humans savages, barbarous or using any other ludicrous names is a crime that should be tolerated, no matter how big, mighty or famous one might be.

It is the basest of all crimes, and next to murder it is the second in rank for it kills and destroys all that is genuine and alive, a crime that we should all avoid, for disrespect has no place in an objective intellectual mind, it reveals the hidden agenda of a racist and genocidal idol, a pitfall and arrogance that not many seem to avoid or notice.

On Holy Wars and Murder

"God made life." Yet, the same person seem to state to know better and take it away before its natural due time.

On Books

I like talking to the dead, this is why I read old books

On Politics

It is like a big pile of manure; wherever you move it, it stinks. You can't make everybody happy, you do what you can and hope for the best.

The Insider

Who do we talk to when we converse with ourselves?

What do we seek when we look forward in the depth of our minds?

Who answers when we are in doubt even when we thought we never asked?

Who keeps guard when we seem to be reckless yet still in control?

What keeps a tally of memories and what insists on having souvenirs?

Who gave the order to think and never to stop?

What set the motion of echoes into the orbit of us?

Who set the rule that sometimes I shall look but not see?

Why do I find what am not looking for?

What is beyond the unknown Selfdom?

What looks from within to the outside world unfazed?

What craves that which it doesn't know?

How old is the shallow abyss? Who are we not to know?

If thoughts are invisible, how come I can see them?

How come we lie to ourselves or is it the self that lies to us?

If we are to end how come we continue?

If the sun is a lonely star, how come I shine in the darkness?

If we can't why we did?

If each one is only once one of a surging kind, why is it that I remember the lives of others?

On Devine Endorsement

God does not need endorsement, yet isn't that what all religions are about?

On the Eloquence of Pictures

A picture can utter nothing to describe itself

My Passage

The journey was not easy, but it was not hard as for some it was, and will be

I am not telling a story for I am recounting what according to me happened

I am not expecting sympathy for I know it is a fading

I am willing to concede, but I will never give up

I may crawl sometimes, but I will never kneel for I am free

I refuse fear for into death I meet the fate of my friends and family

On Having an Open Mind

I do not worship, but those that do are not my enemies as we are all not meant to see through the same angle

I hide, as in hiding sometimes there is also wisdom

I speak many tongues by to mine I will always go back, for I intend not to lose myself but to find others

My Lot

I cry for in crying I do remember my loved ones

I am immortal for mortality can no longer kill me; I am neither arrogant nor full of vanity or self-entitlement as I know I will not be remembered

I wish I could linger, but I know I am already gone

On Expedient Moral Chains

I have no honor, but I will not let shame paint my name as I am beyond petty measurements.

The Purpose of the Past

We sometimes teach the past to forget the present

Being Immutable

I speak in an ancient tongue that carries me through time and back

I need no imagination or artifacts for the past in me I hold

On Creation

To humankind I bear sympathy, but to the creation I am an eternal admirer.

As I Am

I am not wise for wisdom is the realm of the balanced and unstable. I carry a curse yet I glide in the knowledge of certainty.

On Patriotism and Real Sacrifice

Most people who are so patriotic as to clamor for war, just like most politicians, are people who do not know what it is and have not intention to be part of it in any shape or form; of course, some of them will bear the title of war veterans, but if you look deeply in their past you will find that even in the middle of the battlefields they always chose to stick to a desk.

On Thoughts

You carry your thoughts like some drunk carries a bottle of liquor in one of his side pockets; you are equally dependent on them. Have you ever asked yourself if you really own them?

On Growing Up

I see that you have spent some time now building your home; how much time have you spent rebuilding your mind?

On Discovery

You discover nothing; you only learn of what you have been ignorant of so far.

On the Past and the Future

The past and future do not exist; we euphemistically say that they are, but logic states that the past was and that the future will be.

The past is that which cannot be changed and the future is a construct, a sham; the first step and cover for every scam.

Both were crafted by humankind to hide its hollow reasons and to justify all that is not and should not be.

The tyranny of both does doom every human being to be robbed of life's potential; becoming a hostage of powers beyond one's control.

Courage

I have been there, I have seen it before

Hear my voice in the dark

I can see your shadow, I also feel the drag

But just like me you will rise

See my rays over the hill

Believe in my promise

I am the sun riding the abyss

I am the voice you hear in your utmost

I am the brightness in the beautiful coast

I am you in a few steps, in a mile; I am you
when you get there as you were

I have been there all along

I feel the cold bruising your face

The ground burying your feet

You feel sinking, but trust me you are not

You are that glimpse adjusting to the light

If all fades remember you are all that was left

Bad Habits of Some of the Rich and Poor

Some of the rich have the habit of dividing to conquer; some of the poor generalize to be duped better.

On the People

Ah! The people! Formed, deformed, welded and disassembled; in short, invented from scratch. The people are a myth and do not exist; unfortunately for them they are the only ones not knowing it.

On Unsolicited Confidences

One must pay meticulous attention to the private confessions of the wolf.

On the Scoundrel's Kindness

Being charitable with the money of others is the purview of the imbecile and the deceitful.

On Myths

What is the raison d'être of a myth? It is not to explain a problem, but to hide a truth.

On the Human Folly

In the human folly, no one has the monopoly of the abyss; we all have the devil in the depth of our hearts and sometimes you don't need to do much to make him burst out.

On the Lack of Imagination

There are moments when we cannot see, and other moments when we do not see enough; the lack of imagination is crueller than the lack of spirit as it is total blindness.

On Living

Living means to struggle, but it also means living!

On Passions

Passions are that mysterious mechanism which drives us to live.

Our Common Enemy

The poor are those that slave their lives away; the system has absorbed them so utterly that they do not see it anymore. Our tyrants living under the shackles of the same system, which they inherited, are not in possession of their humanity.

On Political Thievery

The illustrious thieves: not serene enough to seek their fortune bravely and equally not intelligent enough to win it honestly.

Death Toll

The placid icy death does cause havoc only where light is the most obscure, more restrained, more wretched, there where the heart ceases to beat under the terrible charge of incomprehension.

The Hidden Aim of Truth

"Expired exalted spirits" is the goal of every truth.

On Hate Hour

Societies that preach hate are where people no longer know how to live.

On the Perception of Corruption

Corruption is a driving force, when it is perceived in a society, for it creates doubts and by that liberates the spirit off the chains of certainty; one starts to think and question.

On Tombs

The tomb, what is the tomb? Is it that terrible? The tomb, all the same, is the residence of the beloved grandfather; of a parent whom we terribly miss and look forward to perhaps reunite with one day.

Isn't the tomb the residence of all those beings that made our lives joyous? No, the tomb, if it is not advantageous for us, should not scare us; since the tomb is the future of humankind, I wonder where does this fear and loathing towards our destiny come from?

On Suicide

Suicide is the last attempt of re-emergence of the will of life.

On Beatitude

"Do you believe in God?"
"Yes"
"And you?"
"No, but I think that you should smile."
"Why?"
"Because, within the realm of your knowledge, you should know that there's a benevolent God looking at you."

On War Campaigns

Soldiers pumped up with fear and armed with weapons unleashed on earth.

On Honesty

Honesty is the gallows of oneself and the intimate being in us, but it is also a blessing and an amnesty for the destitute passerby.

On Wars as Human Sacrifices

The whole world is but appeasing the oriental daemons as Moloch still reigns supreme; this is one of the main reasons for war.

Defining Death

Death is never the cemetery, never is the tomb,

Death is, why should I define it I who is already dead? Death is the surrounding areas, the neighborhood, it is everywhere.

The Brave's Achilles' Heel

Incompetence is the weakness of the brave.

Being Thankful

Just like the ingrates, mediocre people do not know how to be grateful.

On Gratitude

Gratitude is the sublime art of respect.

On Disrespect

It is not by insulting people that we teach them.

On Arguments and Taste

When we are wise we resort to arguments, however when we lack imagination we resort to one's taste.

On Suspicious Minds

He who sees the world as ugly does limit it.

He who sees the world unlimited tries to embellish it and does not see evil in it.

He who lacks imagination will always distrust life and a prison for him it will be.

To the Politically Correct

You tell the truth with an all Roman Republic honesty! This means very little.

Love's First Condition

"How can we love others if we don't love ourselves?" Said the self-radiating sun.

On Stereotypes and Sweeping Statements

"They are all the same!" Is the cruelest gallows humankind ever built.

On the Free Will Argument

The free will argument is religion's way of saying that God offers no warranty for his creation.

Thinking as A Remedy

It is only when humankind starts to think its pain that it will learn something.

On the Absurdity of the World

Intelligence finds the world absurd, yet it never ceases to be surprised by it!

On Memory

Memory is the most misleading of all human tools; it is short sighted and pretends to reign with no somnolence.

Memory never lies, but it does not always tell the truth.

World History

World history, just like our present, stinks of death, rotten corpses, foul crimes, and both are mostly chronicled by the savages and the murderers; know this bleak and criminal neighborhood, and stay away if you can.

Empathy for the Gods

What I do not like about the gods is that they are very resentful; is this due to their humanity?

On a People's Indecision

The indecision of a people is its certain death. It is as dangerous as the indecision of a swimmer amid a shipwreck or lethal currents, worst it is the bleating, the recklessness of the mouton in front of the approaching wolves.

On the End of Free Will

When the absolute free will argument loses its shining armour, we are left with one unsettling conclusion; there is but circumstantial free will.

On the Bailout of Banks

There is nothing more absurd than a bank looking for money, yet here we go again.

Our Current Predicament

Those that can fight are blind

Those that know won't fight

Those that don't know just follow

Those that witness are afraid to speak

Those that are mute they just can't

Those that will run can't hide

Those that hide are not worth looking for

All that is left is you and I, and I think they are getting closer

Silence

On Being Pragmatic

"But dear philosopher if we only were able to read and write!" Said the hopeful mind.

"If only we knew how to listen for then the goal would be reached!" Said the philosopher with a sigh.

On the Devine Origin of Humankind

You always end up insulting humankind if you continue to accord to it, even as a compliment, qualities of other creatures.

You inevitably misread the Divine by giving credit to organized religion's claims of being its inspiration.

You always end up not seeing humankind for what it is by giving its follies a divine purpose.

On the Importance of Self-Evaluation

You have to analyze yourself before others do, because when they do they may find you wanting and they'd be right.

On Narcissism

The most famous and beloved of all the gods of the rich and the people, for indeed they do have a common god, is the bovine god called vanity.

On Worshiping Idols

If the people persist in making idols, it is in order to amuse themselves in destroying them later; the people are the eternal child.

On Being Out of Reach

I am a ghost for I never was haunted or misled by gravity.

Beyond Religion

Religion is the limit; beyond it is wisdom, but also the uncertain.

On Listening

Sometimes charity is also listening to someone talk about something you don't approve of, just because he or she needs the conversation more than you do.

On the Disposition of Nemesis

One must be thankful for not having the personality of his enemies for they help him identify what one is not; they are not the reflection, but the reverse of our identity.

The Secret of Creation

An old man was walking up a hill pushing his old wife, a very thin woman, on a wheel chair.

A wise man saw the scene and asked himself, "Is he wheeling her up or down?"

A fool walking by saw the same scene, and thought, well he did not think of anything, he just walked on.

A scientist, looking out of a window, said to his students that the old man was pushing his way up and is certainly being pulled down.

A vigilante, raising an eyebrow, and piercing the scene with his watchful eyes, outraged by such a blatant public display and disregard of the law, picked up a communication device to report a man not using the sidewalks.

A banker, in an important meeting, lecturing his staff, paused, viewing the scene from his glass tower, whispered to himself, "Interests rates should be increased!"

The angels in heaven watched the scene and wondered if this is what the lord intended.

A spirit, sitting nowhere and everywhere asked, "Do old people finally know the secret of creation?

ABOUT THE AUTHOR

Lamine Pearlheart is an avid reader and, as far as he remembers, he always had a great appreciation for literature, history, philosophy, poetry, and enjoys long walks as a meditation form.

He also has a passion for languages; he speaks English, French, German, Spanish and Portuguese.

One of his chief interests is the understanding of the human experience in its multidimensional aspects as is apparent in his books.